The Art of Caro

20 single-sided
adult coloring designs
for
fun & relaxation!

Carolyn V. Hamilton

Swift House Press
Las Vegas, Nevada

Swift House Press
7380 S. Eastern Avenue, Suite 124-216
Las Vegas, Nevada 89123 USA

First North American Edition October 2015

ISBN 978-0-9909664-5-6

Introduction

Welcome to *The Art of Caro.*

Caro is multi-media artist and designer, Carolyn V. Hamilton. She began her commercial art career in the late sixties, the era of *Mad Men.* (When the art department was called "the bull pen" because commercial artists were predominantly men.)

At Los Angeles Trade-Technical College, she learned the tools and vocabulary for preparing artwork and illustration for printing and the printing processes, and earned her A.A. In Commercial Art.

During her professional career as a commercial artist and graphic designer she learned the techniques of several artistic mediums: watercolor, gouache, oil pastels, oil paints, collage, and colored pencils.

Each of these complex and intricate coloring pages is hand-drawn, which means no computer vector graphic software has been used.

Because of this there may be minor imperfections. "I see this as a reflection of real life…where nothing is particularly perfect," she says.

Growing up in rain-soaked Seattle, Caro learned to play quietly in her room, which often involved her favorite pastime, coloring. You can enjoy hours of stress-free fun right now. Don't save it for a rainy day!

At the end of this book, Caro shares with the language of color and how to choose your color palette, how best to use her favorite medium, colored pencils, and *10 Tips and Tricks.*

Every Caro design is an original, hand-drawn work of art. You won't find anything like these designs anywhere else.

How best to render these designs

Each design in *The Art of Caro* is single-sided, so that whatever medium you choose for your colors, they won't bleed through to the next page. However, to be safe, especially if you are using gel pens, you may want to slip a blank piece of paper behind the page you're working on.

Coloring is an endeavor that is both fun and creative. Coloring is also relaxing and calming. And it is said that coloring before bedtime can even ward off insomnia! You can expect hours of stress-free pleasure from this book.

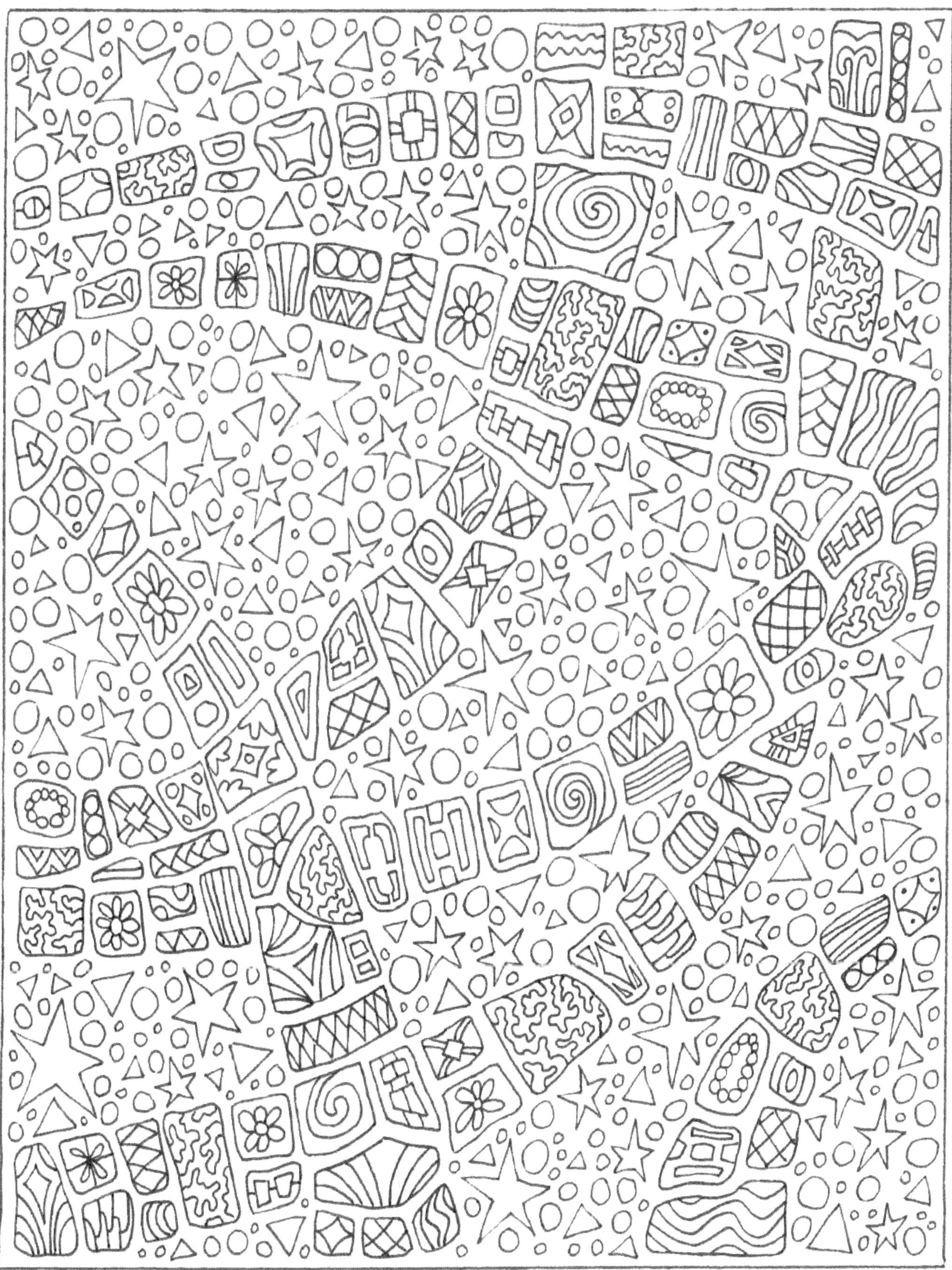

Starburst

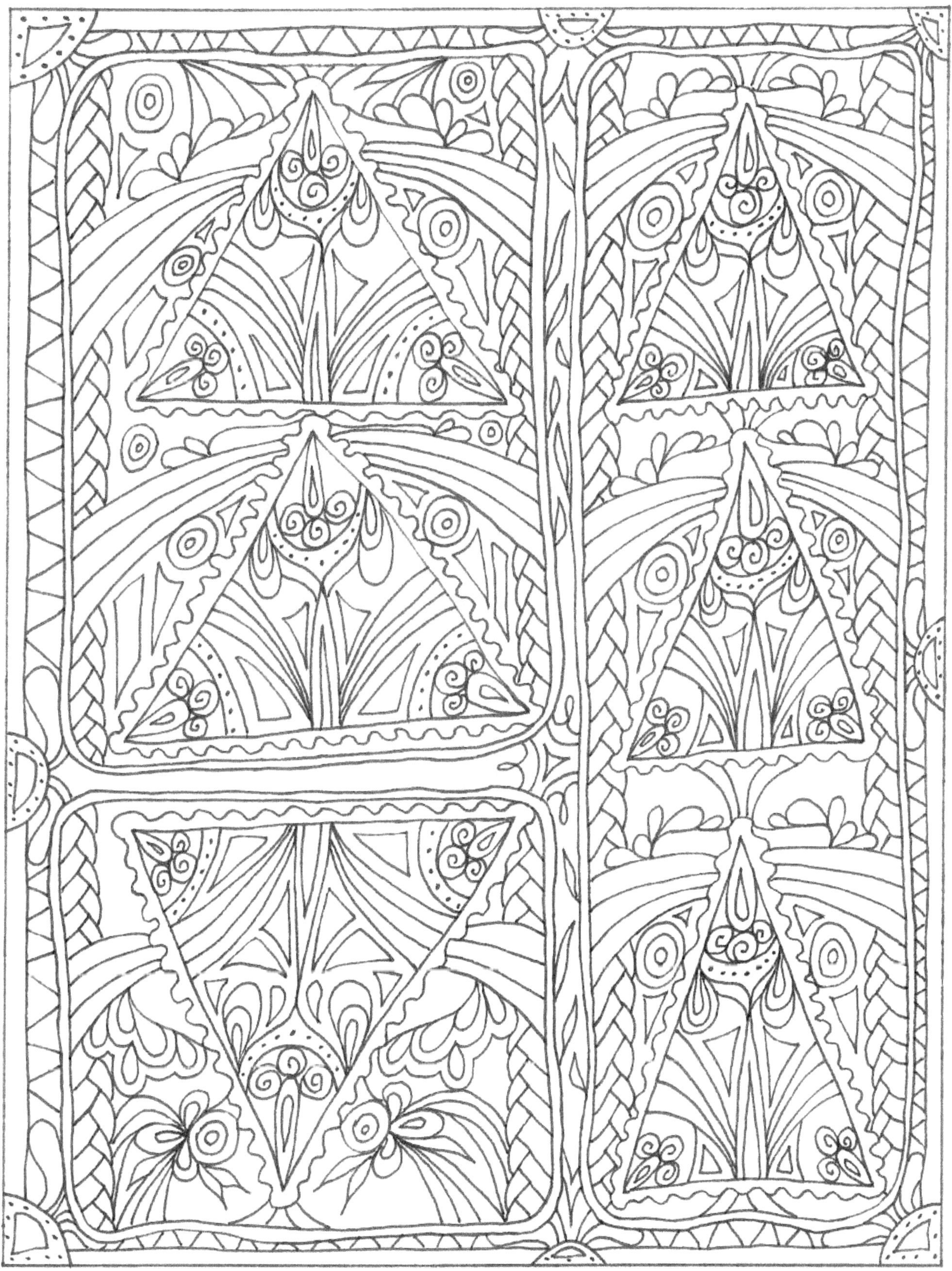

Expectations

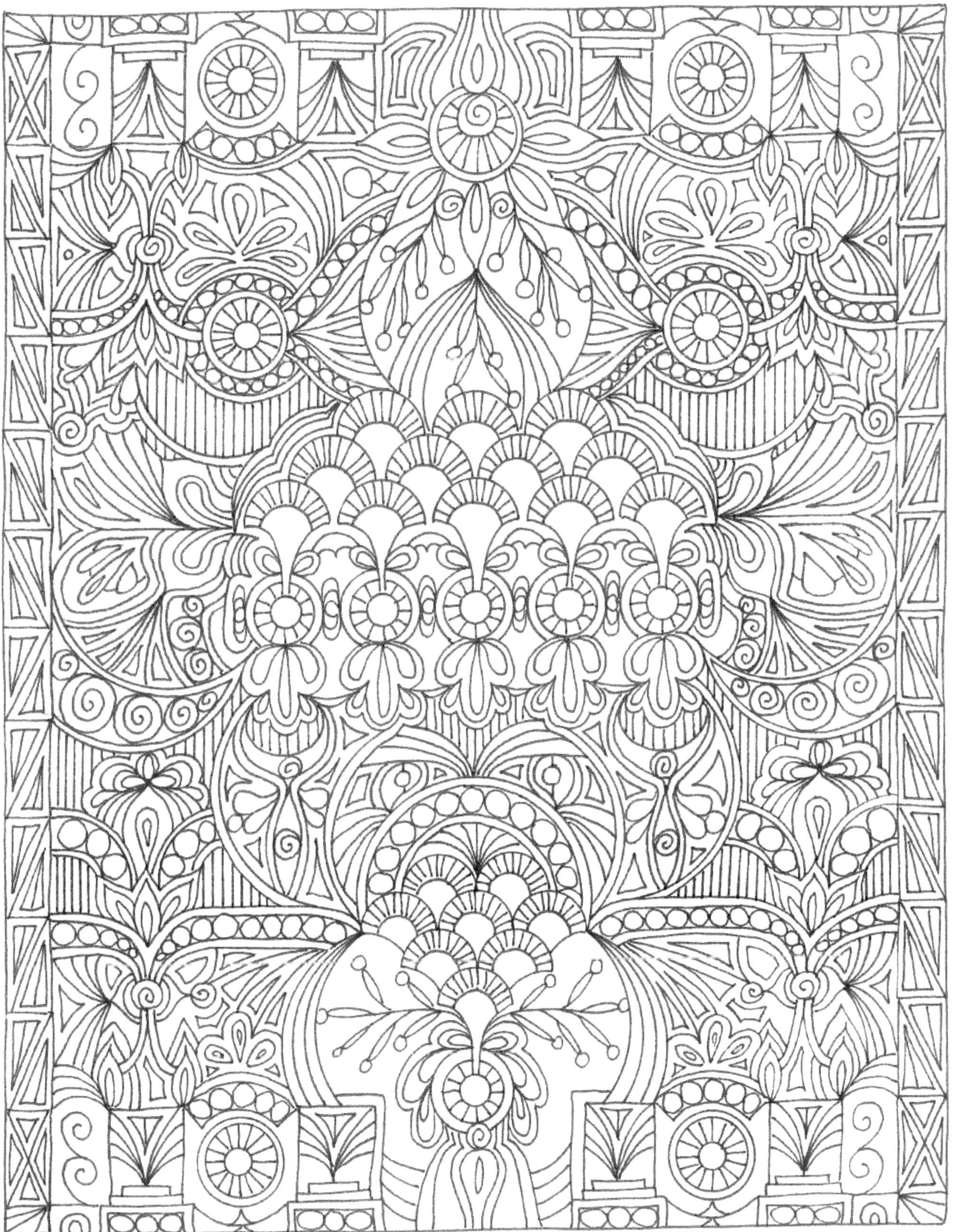

Topkapi

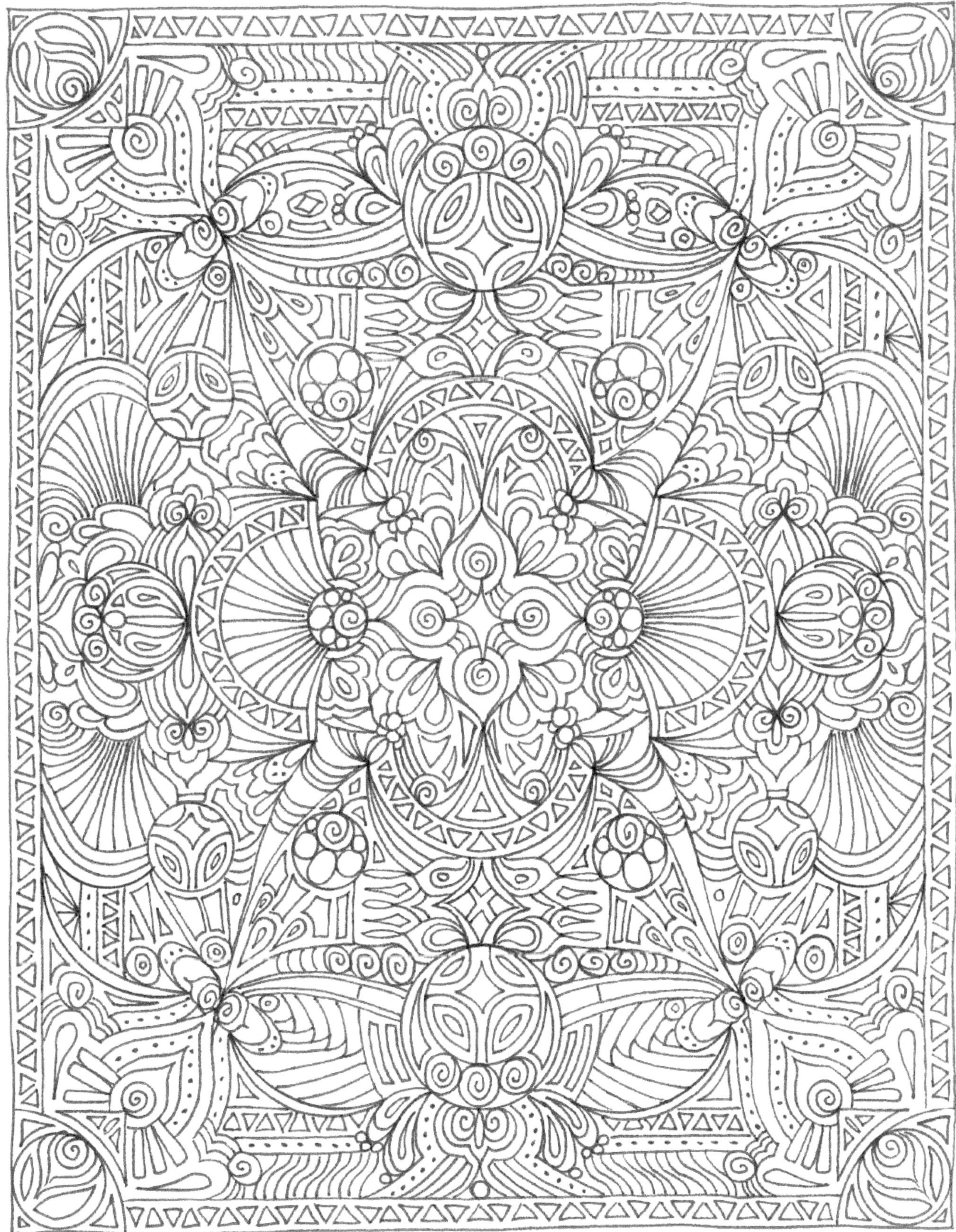

Anatolia

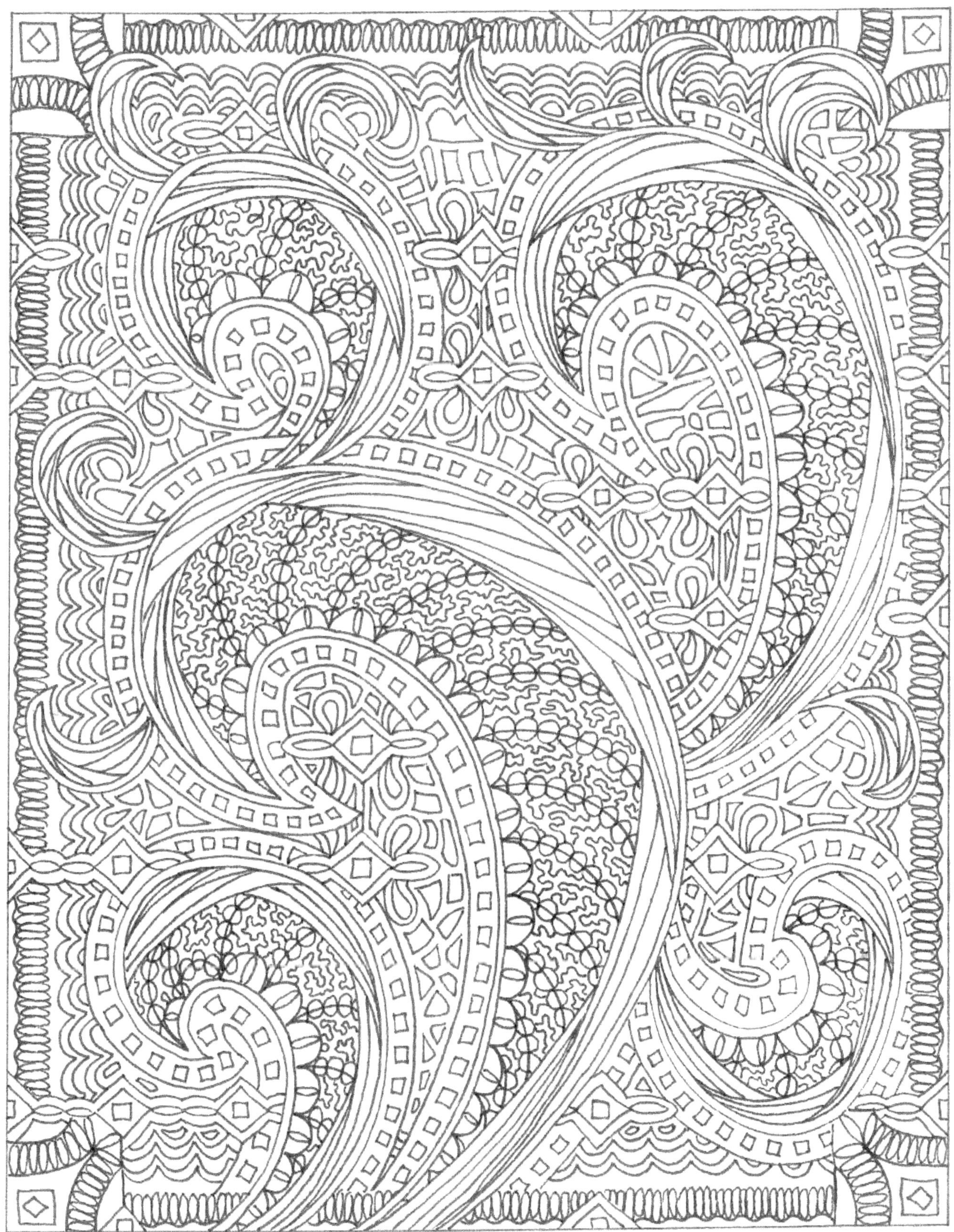

Paisley Zentangled

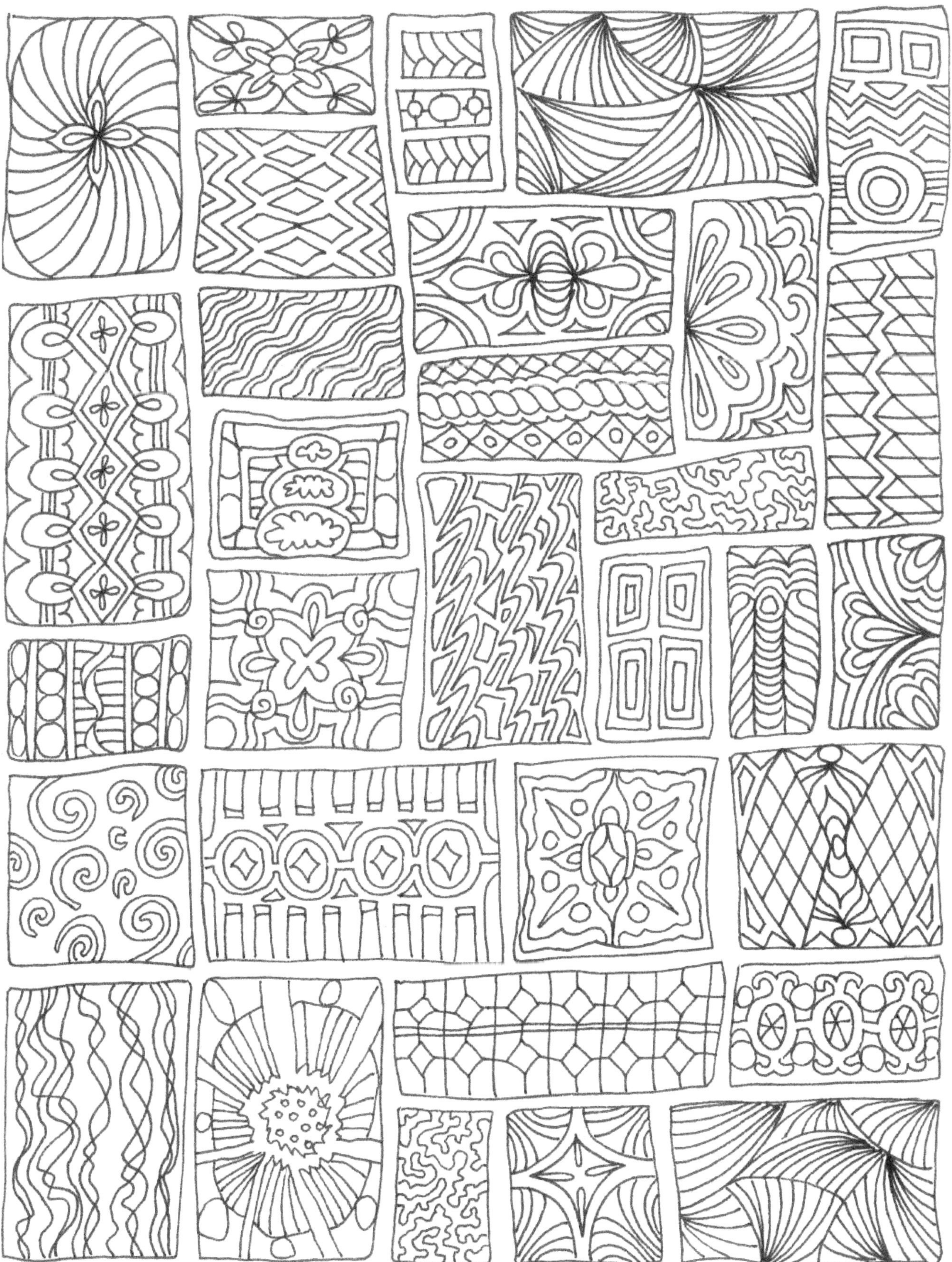

The Tile Wall

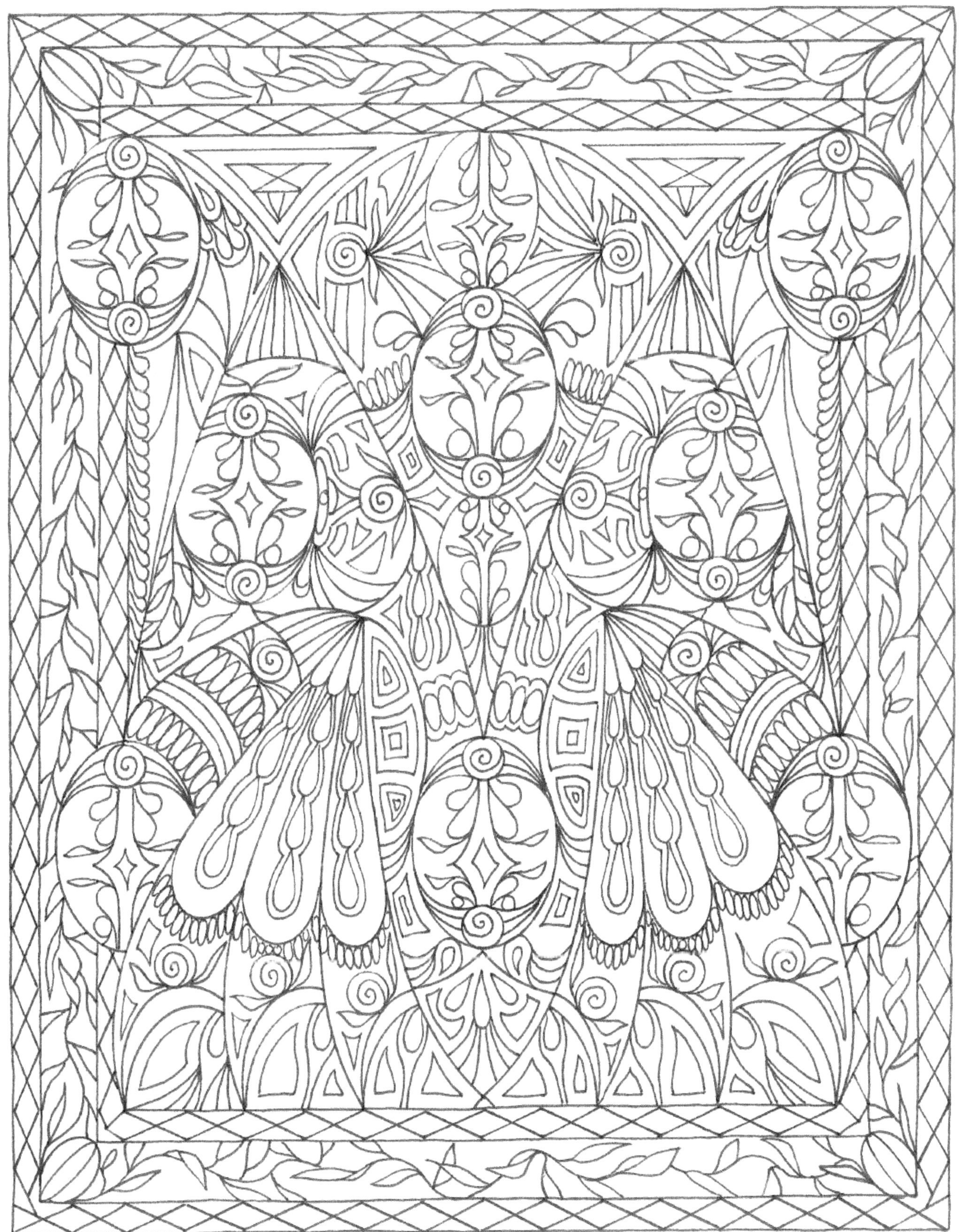

Sumo

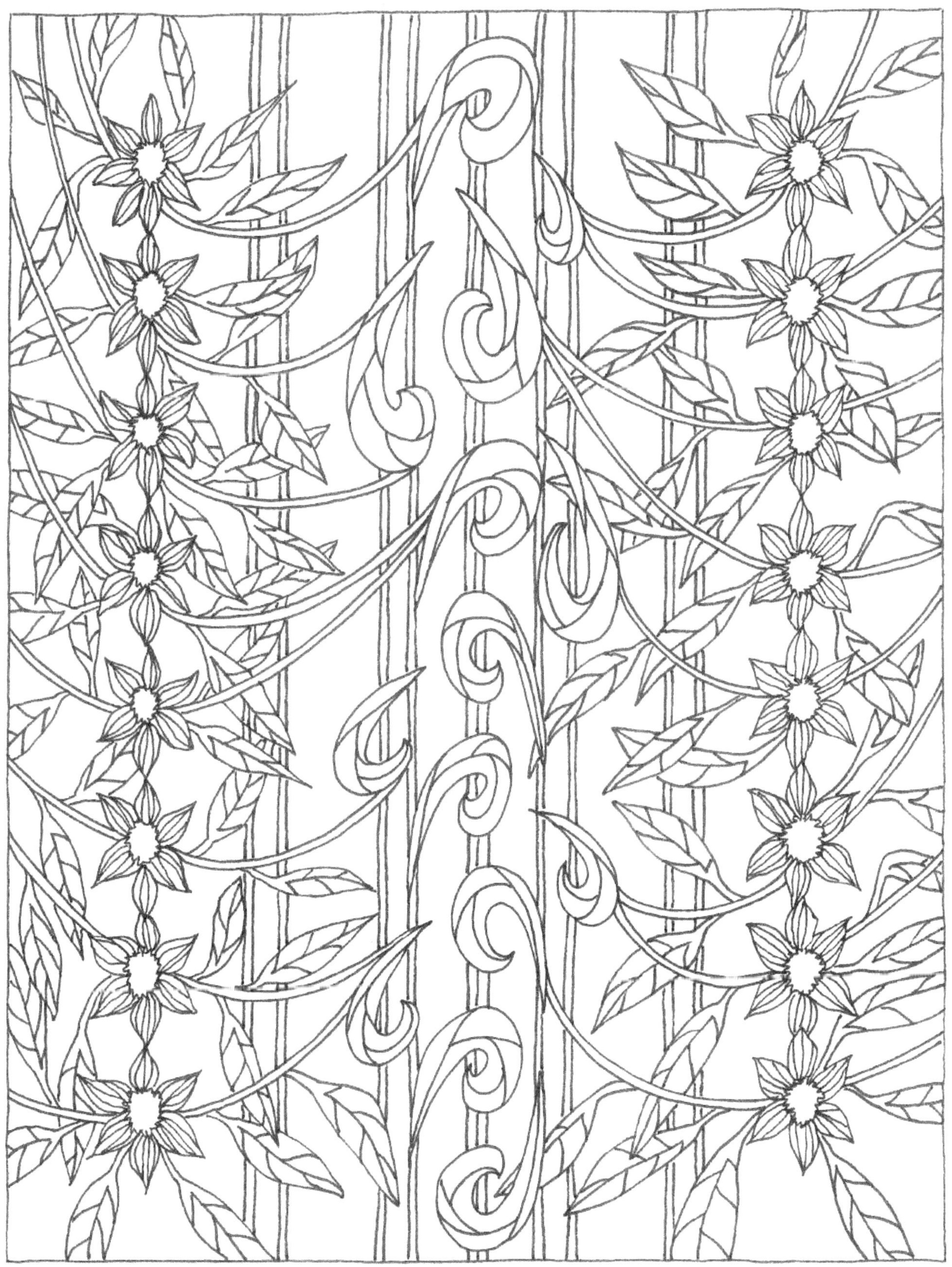

Daffodils

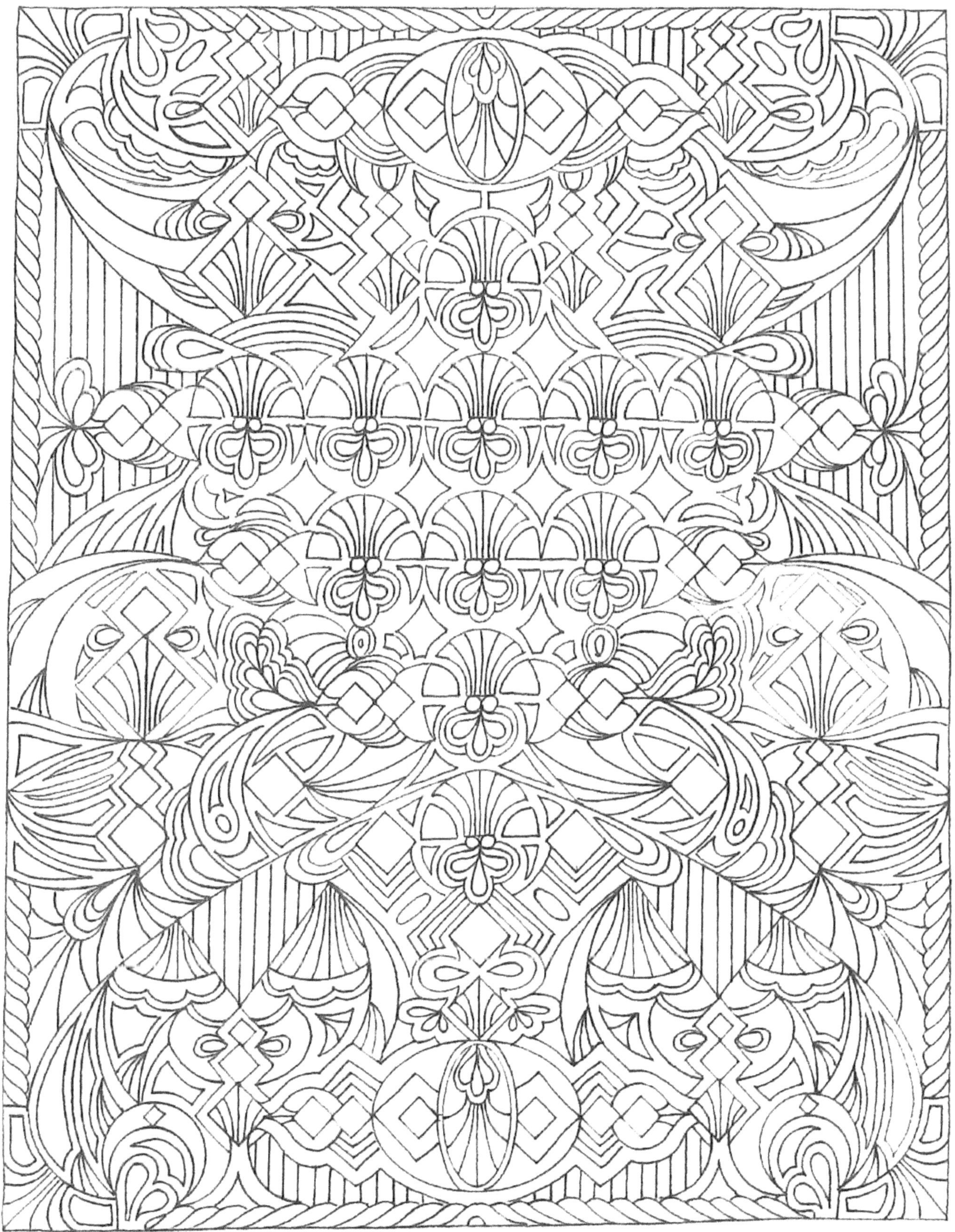

Theater Curtain

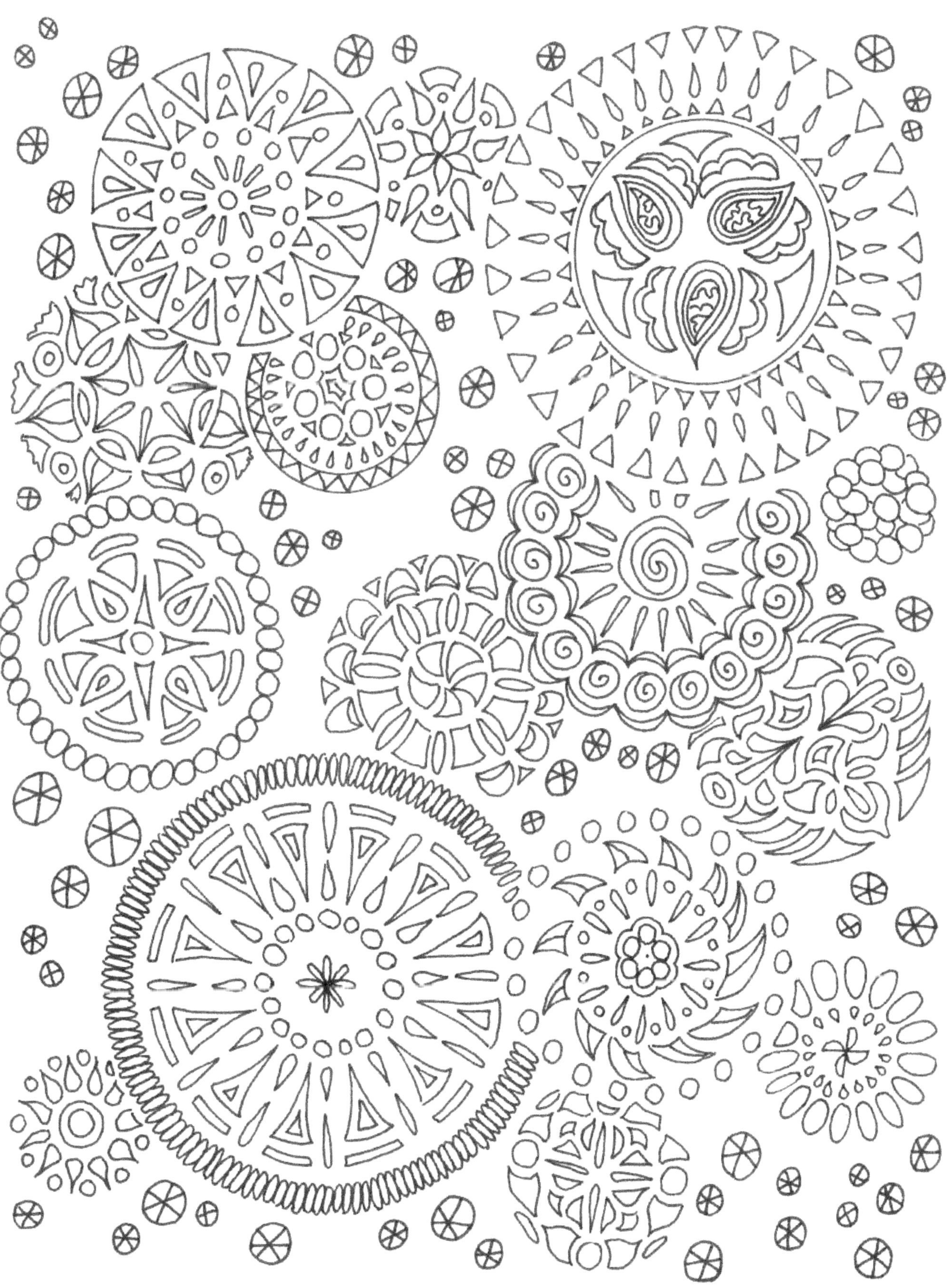

Around We Go

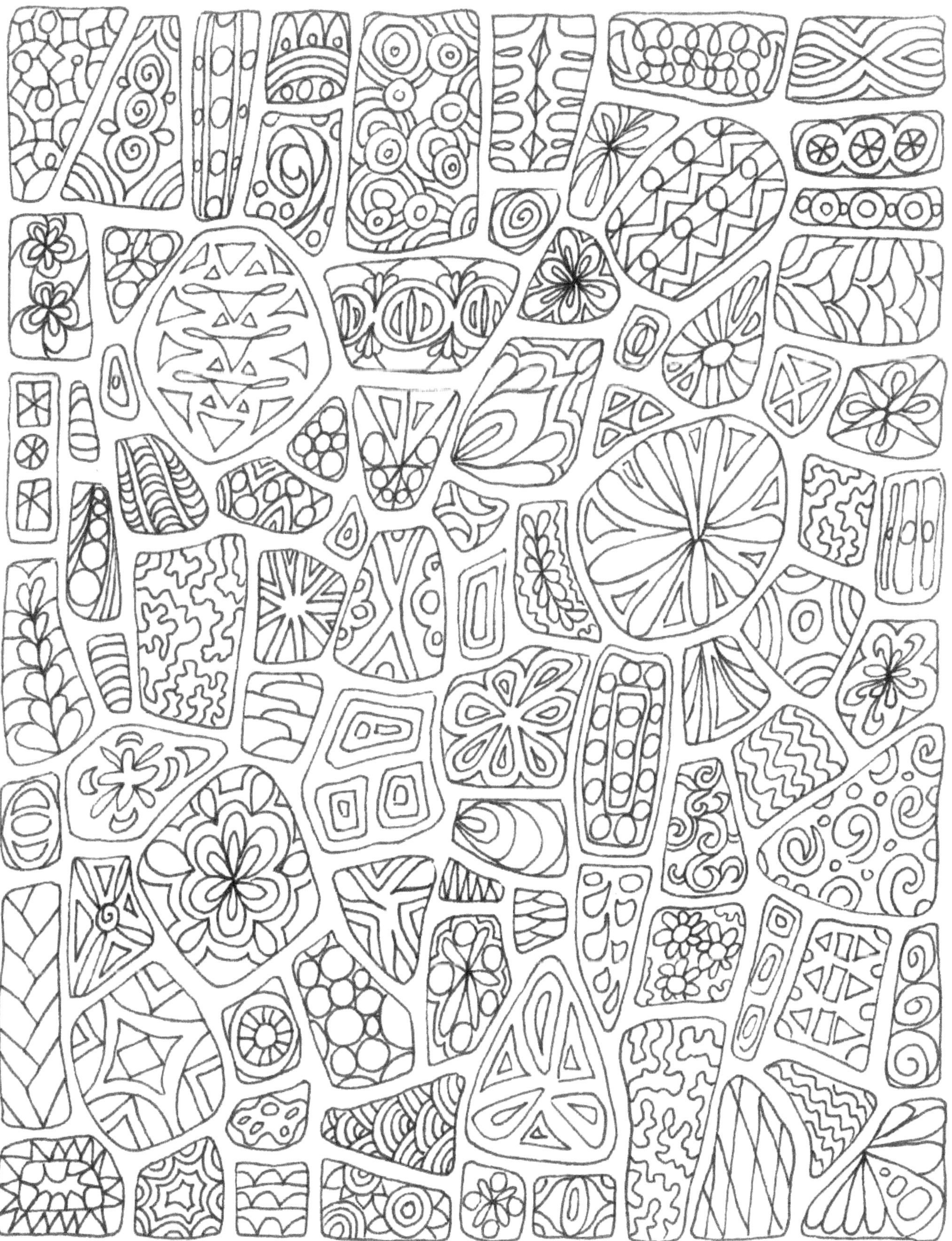

Traveling

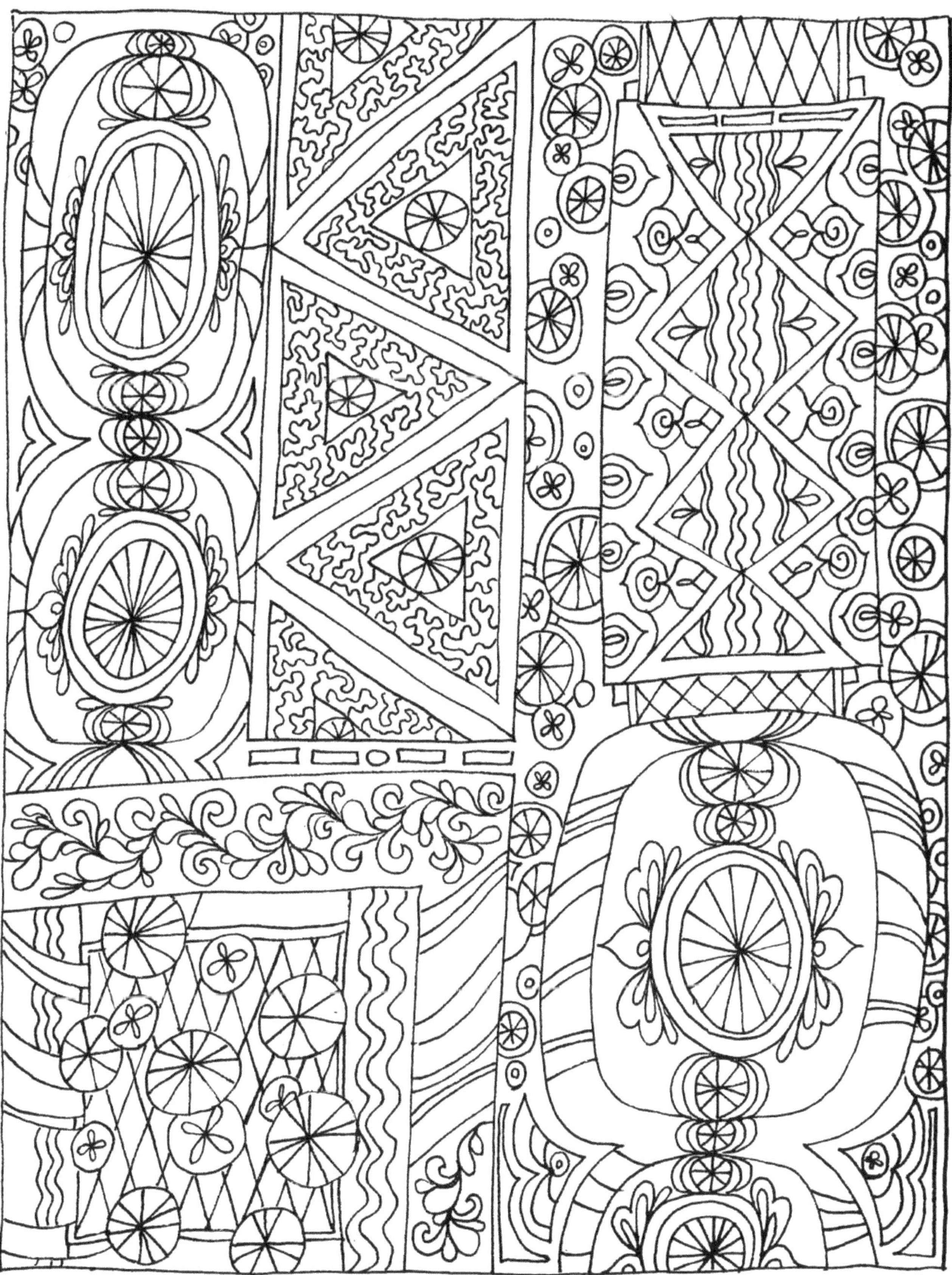

Christmas Candy

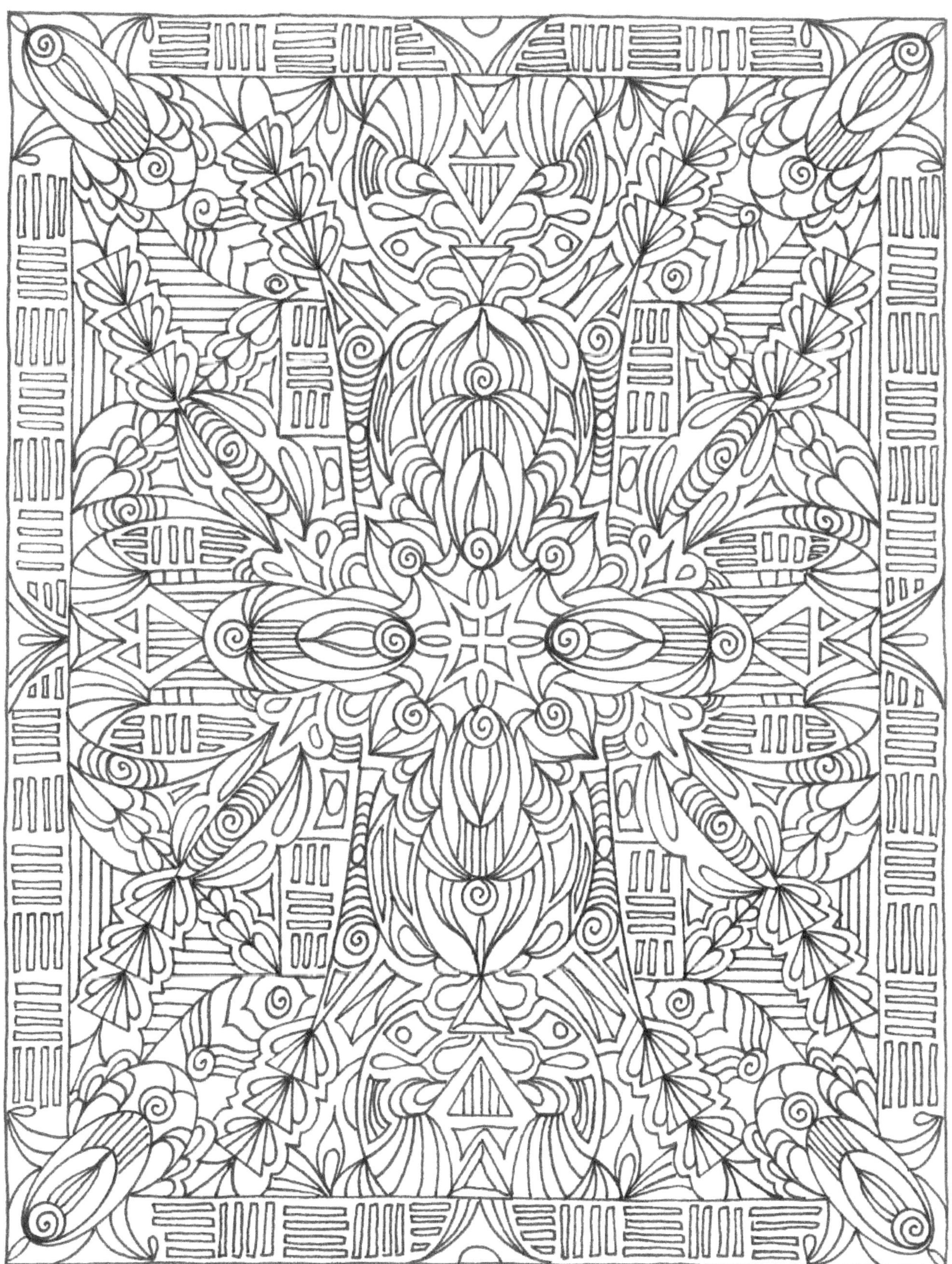

Bamboo

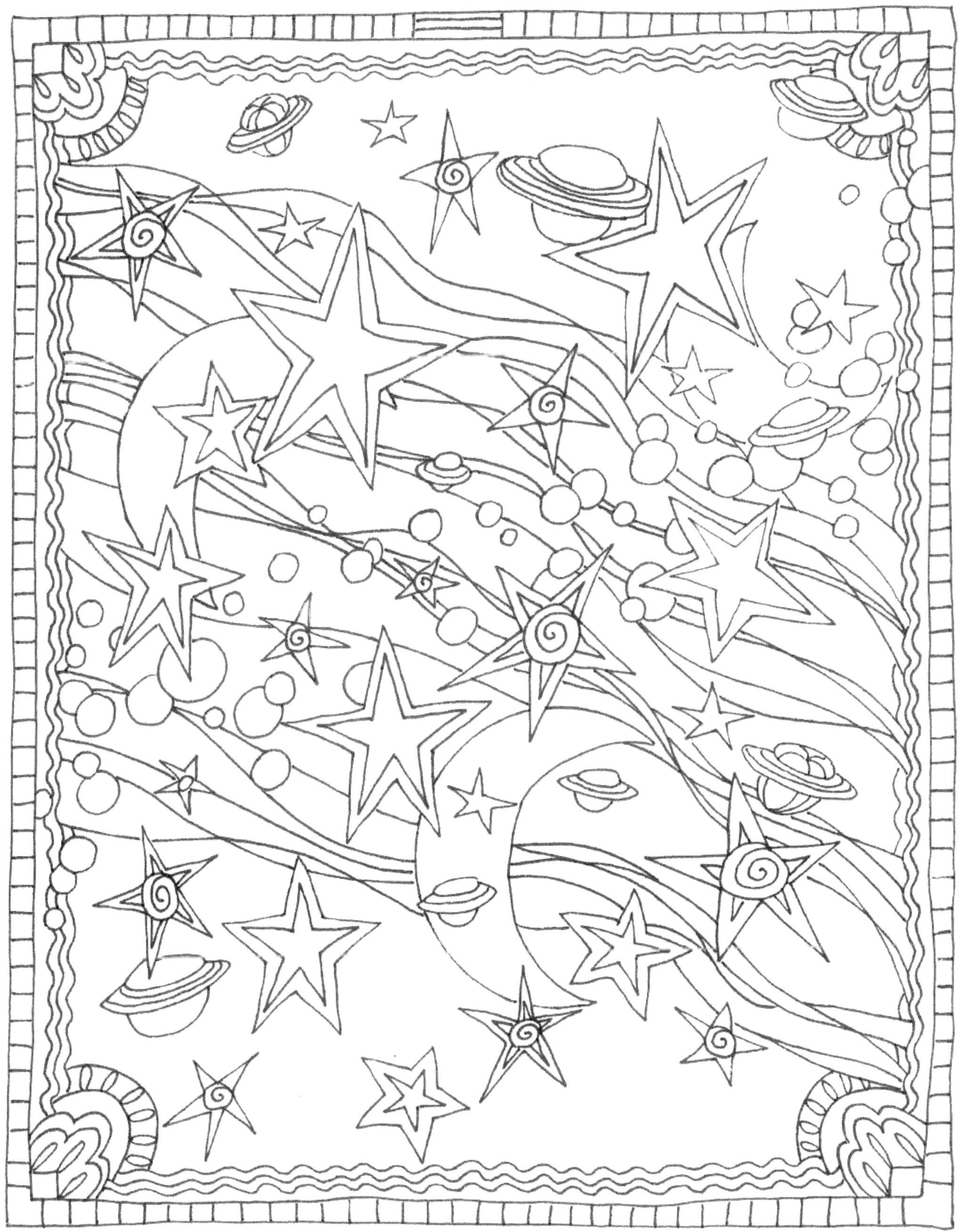

Star Stream

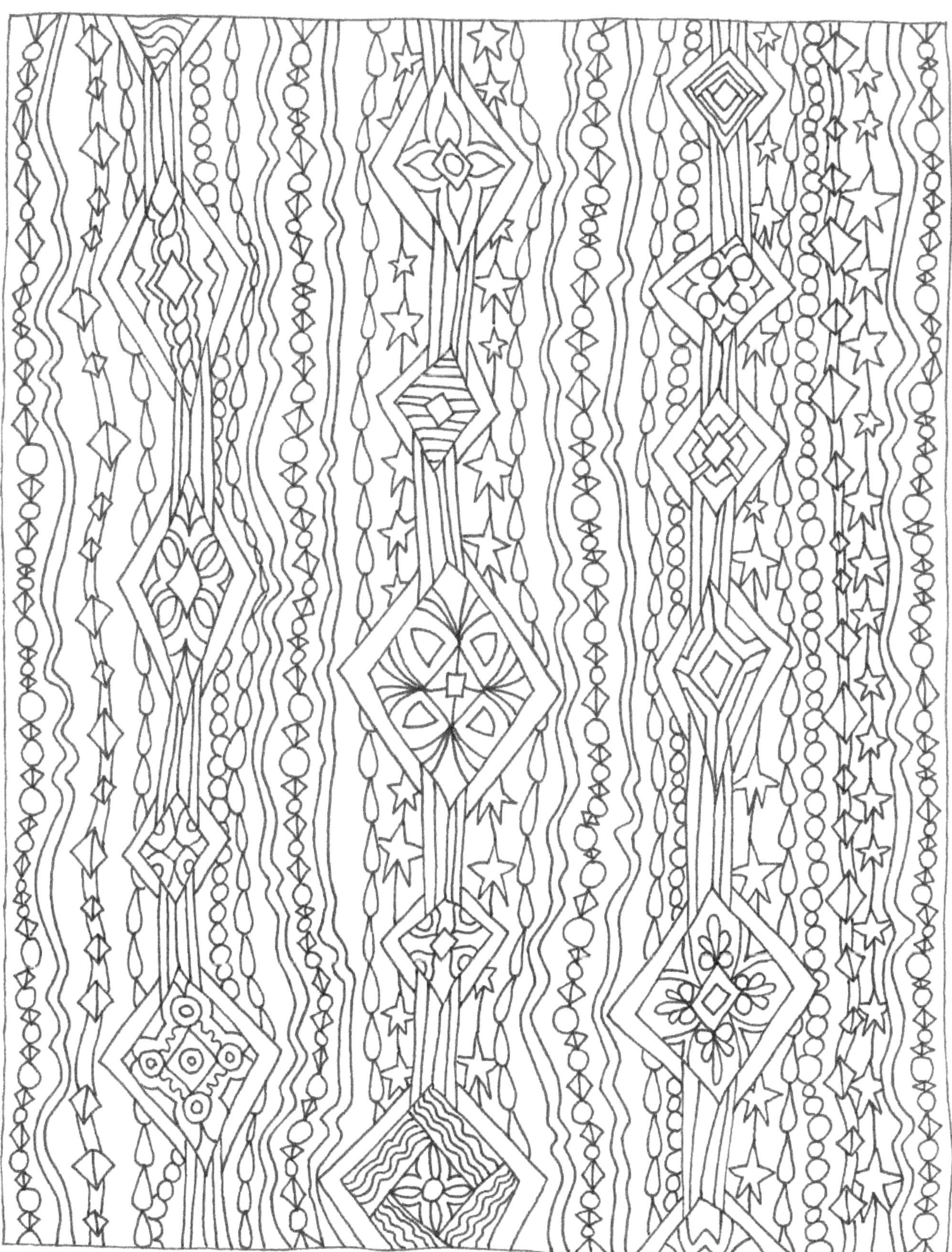

Beadaholic

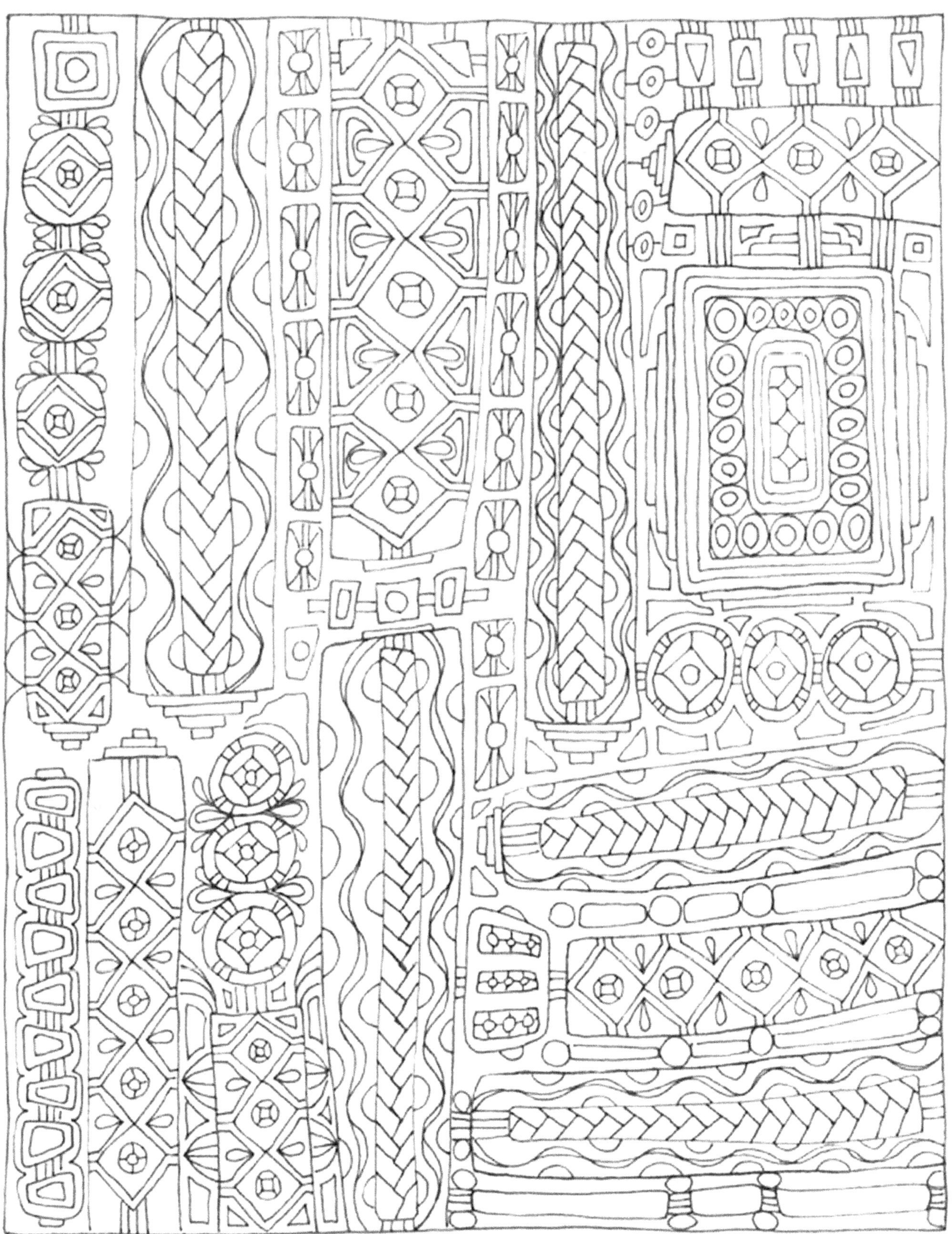

Braided

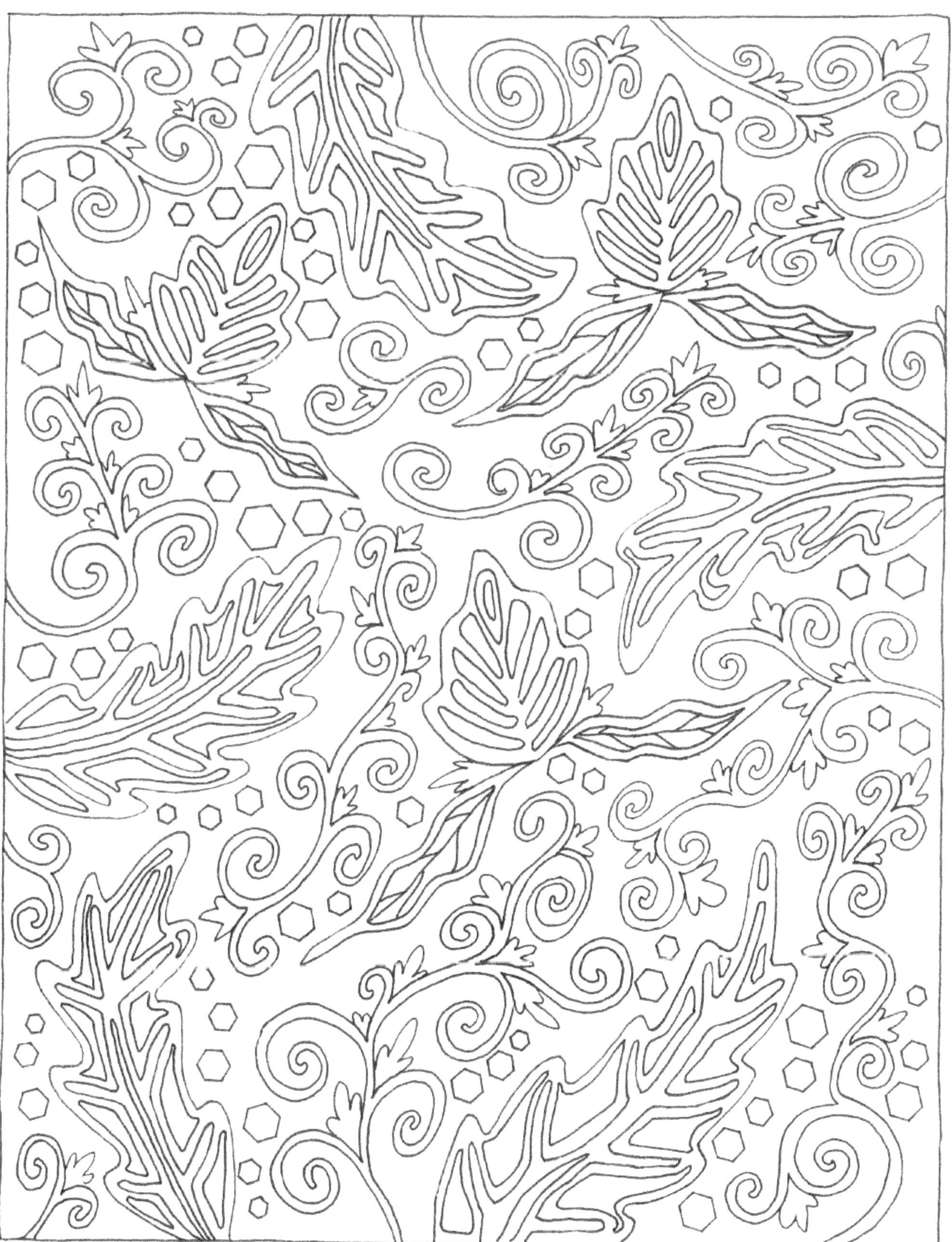

Brocaded

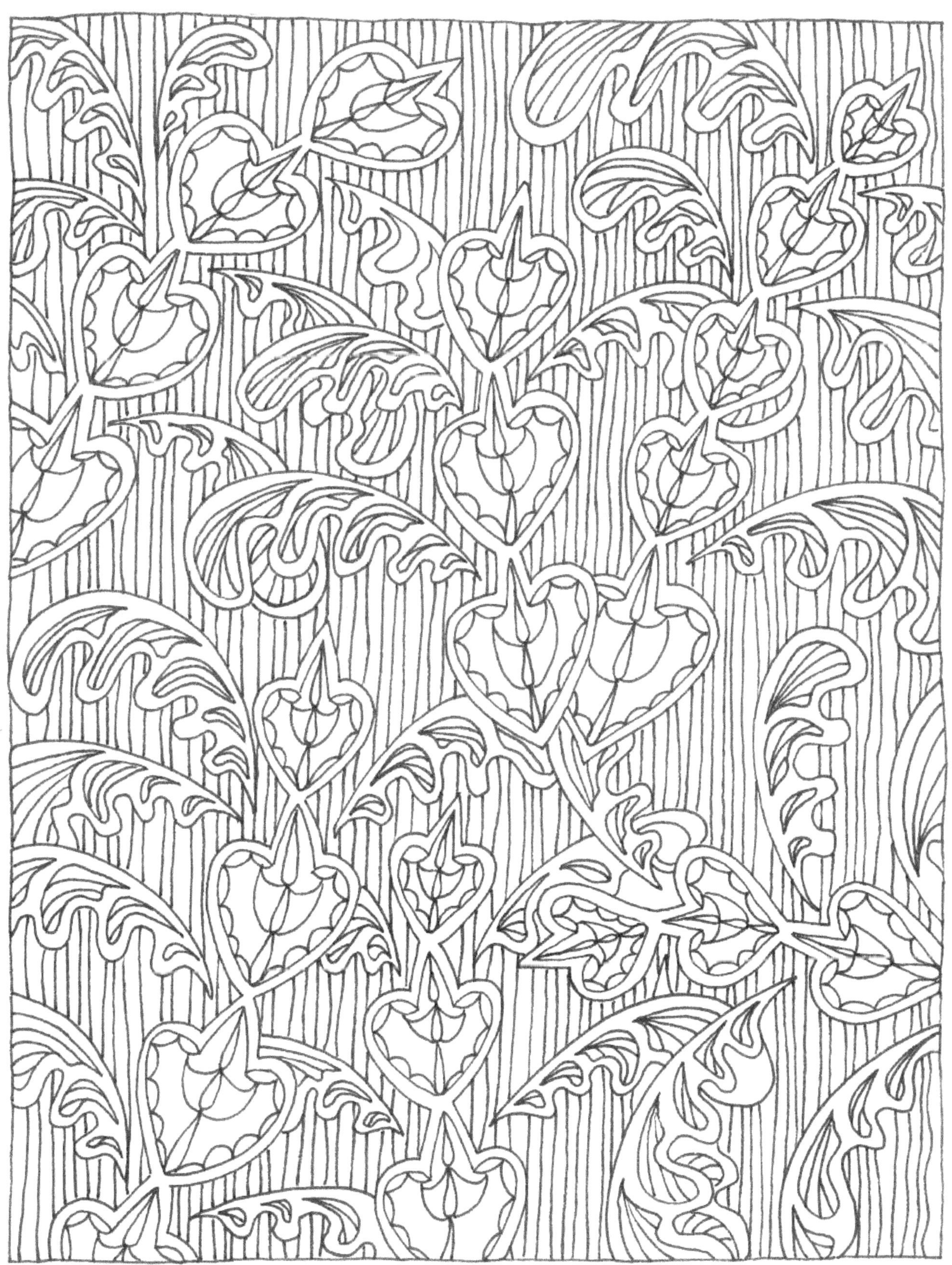

Wallpaper

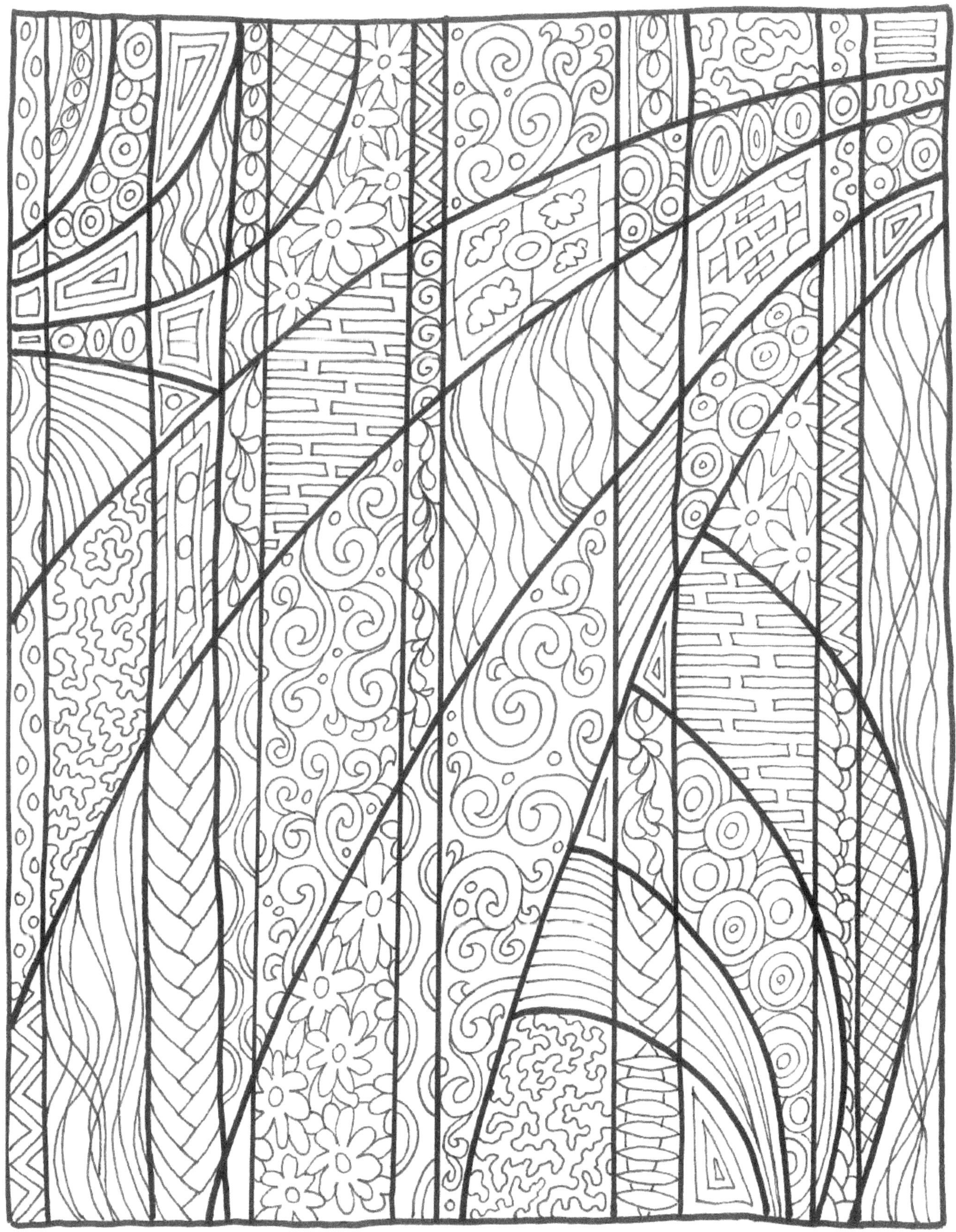

Zentangled

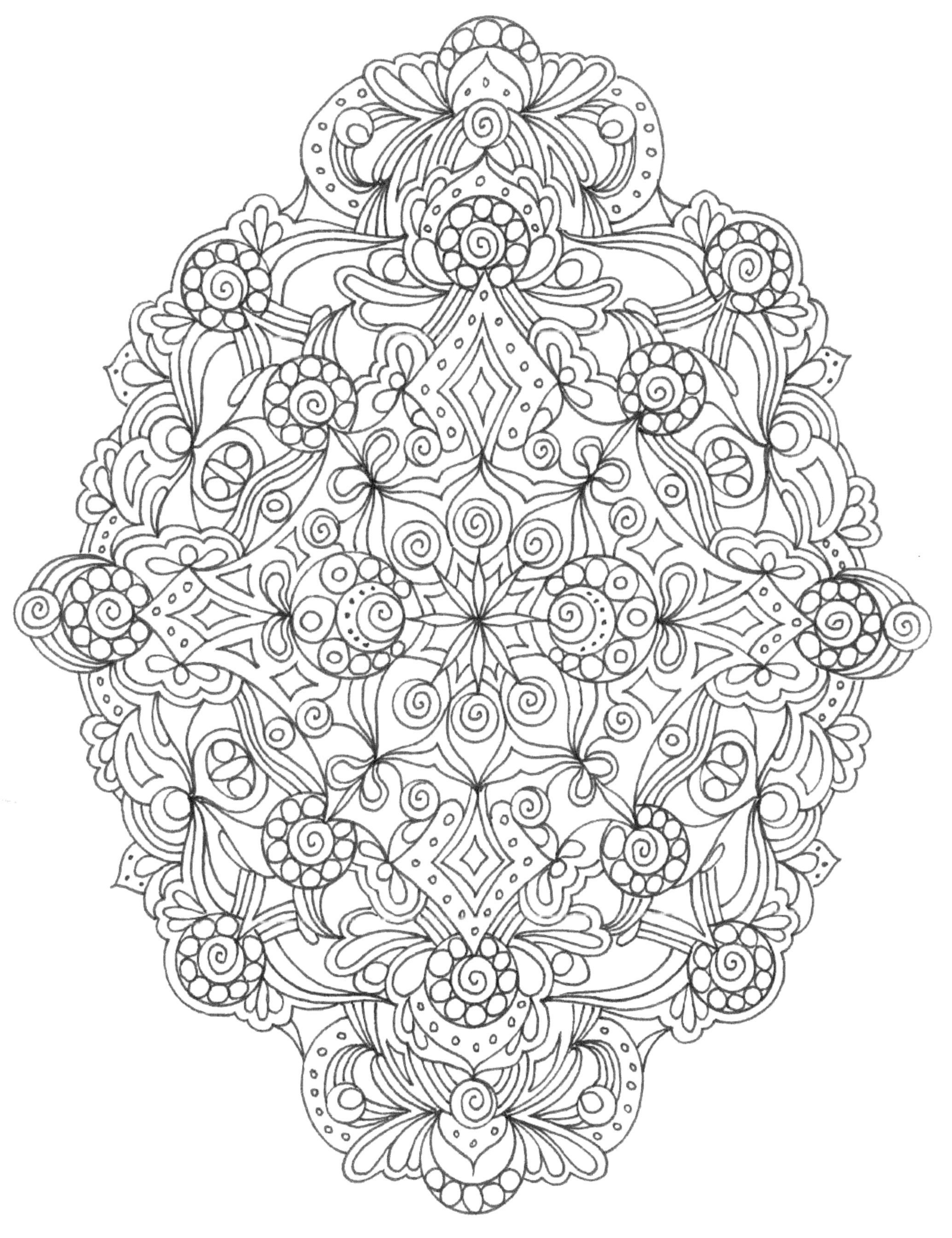

Thunder

BONUS INFORMATION!

What coloring medium will you choose?

Colored pencils or gel pens or a combination of both will be your best choices for rendering these intricate designs.

On using colored pencils

Today's colored pencils have a history of relationship with crayons. Wax-based colored pencils allow you to achieve the color intensities of crayons themselves. They have excellent hue-saturation and strength of color that does not deteriorate with age.

My favorite colored pencils are made by Prismacolor. There are two different kinds for you to explore. For thin line work, the Prismacolor Verithin has a hard lead and they hold their sharp tip longer. When you want a thicker line and heavy shading, the regular Prismacolor pencils are best.

Because these are wax-based pencils, over time they may develop a whitish film called "wax bloom." There are special fixatives to arrest this, or you can just use hair spray. Be aware that any fixative you use, even if it's marketed as "odor-less" will release chemicals into the air. Therefore, use fixatives sparingly and in a well-ventilated room.

I love the tactile feeling of the waxy lead moving on the paper.

On using gel pens

Because of their recent artistic popularity, most art and office supply stores now carry gel pens. You can also shop and buy them at amazon.com. Anything from a simple 8-pack to a 96 Gel Pen Set.

Be aware that most gel pens contain a water-based ink. This means you don't want to spill coffee on or otherwise get your paper wet, as the ink will smear.

With gel pens you can create a fine, controlled line. They are also less prone to bleed through to the other side of the paper. However, to be safe, you may want to slip a blank sheet of paper behind the one you're coloring.

About colored markers

I do not recommend using colored markers because most of them bleed outside the lines as well as through the paper.

The language of color

Nothing beats the joy of color!

Color is all around us. It can affect how we feel and react. A whole psychology has been built around color and it is often used by interior designers.

Colors can even have different connotations in different cultures. For instance, *white* in our culture symbolizes cleanliness and purity, while in some Eastern cultures white is the color of mourning. In casinos, the felt on blackjack tables is *green* because that is the most soothing color to the eyes, and God forbid a player should leave the game because his eyes are tired!

There is even the holistic use of color—chromotherapy—as a healing therapy which dates back to ancient Chinese and Egyptian cultures.

Whether a color is warm or cool is determined by how much blue or yellow is in it.

The *HUE* refers to the color itself. All hues can be mixed from two of the three basic hues, or primary colors: red, yellow and blue.

Theoretically if all three colors are mixed, the resulting color is black.

The *VALUE* of a color has to do with how light or dark it is.

One of my mentors was artist Mike Miller who in his early days (this is waaaay before digital animation) painted cartoon gels in gouache for Hanna Barbera. He told me to put a warm color such as red or yellow next to a cool color such as blue or green for visual impact.

Your color palette

Color is the inherent factor that will make these designs come alive. Before you begin, you want to consider and select your colors.

You might select a palette of mostly blues and greens for a cool, monochromatic effect. You might choose to add a tiny spot of a warm color to enliven the blues and greens.

A "primary palette" would contain red, blue and yellow. You could include a light red and a dark red, a light blue and a dark blue, and a light yellow and a dark yellow.

Where will this drawing "live" when you are finished? Will it be a gift for someone whose favorite color is magenta? Will you frame it for the wall of your front door entry? Should it match your dining room tablecloth and napkins? The answers to these questions could determine your color palette selections.

For a pleasing color palette I suggest you include at least 6 colors, warm and cool, light and dark. At least 6 colors in your palette will also make coloring these intricate designs easier if you want to be sure each spatial element doesn't "touch" another of the same color.

10 TIPS & TRICKS

1. Wash your hands and use a hand guard. Clean hands mean no grease smudges to discolor the white paper. A "hand guard" is simply another piece of blank white paper that you place under the flat of your hand as you draw. This prevents the natural oils from your skin from smudging the colors or seeping into the paper.

2. If you are working with pencil, find a portable pencil sharpener that contains a reservoir attachment to collect the wood shavings. You'll find that much more convenient than a pencil sharpener you have to carry to the nearest wastebasket to use.

3. For the best results, keep your pencil sharpened so that the color fills the tiniest ridges and valleys of the paper itself. A pencil with a sharp and uniform point will make this easy.

4. For colored pencils, you will experience less lead-breakage if you hold the pencil in a more upright position instead of a 45-degree angle.

5. Work your pencil tip in tiny, circular motions to achieve good tonal application and overall color fill.

6. Heavy burnishing—that is, applying heavy color—will give you the brightest color.

7. Never brush pencil flecks off the page with your hand. Use a soft brush to remove them without accidentally marking the paper.

8. Buy a pencil extender, this little metal gadget encloses the shortest pencil so that you will have continued and comfortable use of it.

9. Have a separate sheet of paper you can place behind the page you are coloring so that gel pens will not bleed through to the next design page.

10. Before you apply a color to your design, test it on another piece of paper to see how you like the final result.

ACKNOWLEDGEMENTS

My artistic influences came from the men I worked for and with during my career as a commercial artist/graphic designer: my first ad agency boss, Art Director Mario Donna, my second ad agency boss Art Director Ed Kelly, Bonanza Printers owner Steve Smith, and Mike Miller, who taught me how to put a warm color next to a cool color for visual impact.

Thank you so much for purchasing The Art of Caro adult coloring book.

Reviews are everything, and if you like the designs here, I would very much appreciate it if you would go to amazon.com and write a review (just a few sentences would be fine) of ***The Art of Caro.***

For more of my original coloring designs, check out my shop at Etsy: www.etsy.com/shop/CaroColoringArt

Also be sure to visit my website, www.CaroColoringArt.com, where I'll be sharing coloring tips, hosting monthly coloring contests and more.

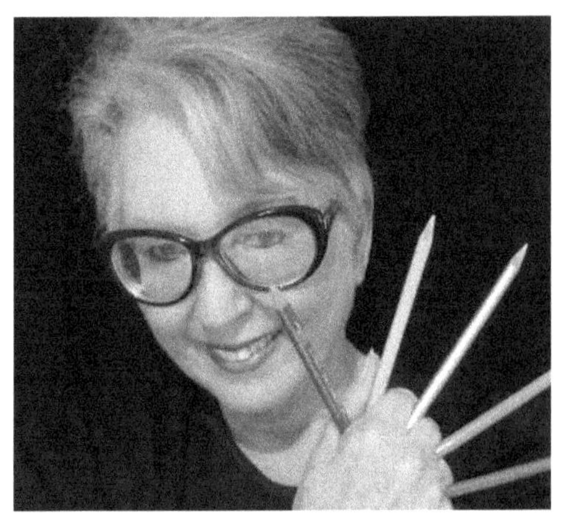

ABOUT THE ARTIST

Carolyn V. Hamilton (CARO) is a published author and retired graphic designer and advertising professional. In her art career, she has created hundreds of logos for businesses and professionals, designed outdoor billboards, and created illustrations for brochures and magazine articles. A graduate of Los Angeles Trade Technical College with an A.A. in Commercial Art, she went on to earn her B.A. in Liberal Arts from Antioch University Seattle. In her "spare time" she has painted portraits in oil on canvas and large interior murals with acrylic paints. In the 1990s she began art journaling during travels around the globe with her actor/comedian husband, Cork Proctor. Now retired to Cuenca, Ecuador, she teaches writing classes as well as art classes. For more information on Carolyn V. Hamilton's fiction and non-fiction books, go to www.carolynvhamilton.com.

If you have any comments, nice or otherwise, on my designs, or any ideas for images you'd like to see, please e-mail me directly at caromodernart@gmail.com

Watch for my next coloring book

Color Caro's

Mystic Mandalas

www.ingramcontent.com/pod-product-compliance
Lightning Source LLC
LaVergne TN
LVHW081325110826
845149LV00007B/1604
* 9 7 8 0 9 9 0 9 6 6 4 5 6 *